Market Yourself!

A Guide to Résumé Creation and Job Search for the Resource Management Professional

By Elizabeth B. Davis, SPHR

Director of Human Resources
APICS Professional Staff

For information:

APICS—The Educational Society for Resource Management
5301 Shawnee Road
Alexandria, VA 22312-2317
Phone: (703) 354-8851
       (800) 444-2742
Fax: (703) 354-8106

ISBN 1-55822-169-7
APICS Stock # 03776   9/99

ABOUT THE AUTHOR

Elizabeth B. Davis, SPHR, is the Director of Human Resources for the professional staff of APICS—The Educational Society for Resource Management (APICS). Ms. Davis joined APICS in 1995 as the Director of Human Resources. She has 20 years of experience as a human resource generalist, with particular skills in recruitment, strategic planning, organizational development, and change management.

Ms. Davis has implemented organizational development initiatives that support customer-oriented, value-based, product-driven operating structures. She has managed change to ensure that customers receive the benefit of high-quality work processes throughout shifts in leadership, product lines, culture, mission, and goals.

Ms. Davis has created and directed the human resources function in corporate and not-for-profit environments. She has managed and executed domestic and international recruitment campaigns in corporate, educational, and high-technology environments. She has overseen policy development and implementation, staff development and training, and review and selection of benefits. She has administered training conferences in Asia, Africa, and Latin America.

Ms. Davis earned an undergraduate degree from Southern Methodist University and a Master of Arts degree from Georgetown University. She is a member of the American Society for Association Executives and the Society for Human Resource Management, from which she earned the credential, Senior Professional in Human Resources.

ABOUT THE AUTHOR

ACKNOWLEDGMENTS

Teamwork is one of the core values of the APICS professional staff. We believe that teamwork has the potential to produce results superior to those achieved by individuals. I have a large team to acknowledge and thank.

First of all, my thanks to the men and women of APICS—The Educational Society for Resource Management. Their commitment to continuous improvement and lifelong learning motivates, educates, and inspires me. Arvil Sexton, CPIM, and Bob Collins, CFPIM, CIRM, brought me face to face with the APICS member communities in their regions; and Richard Meiser, CFPIM, and Wayne Woods, CPIM, provided valuable insights.

I have wanted to put this work together for many years. For their unflagging encouragement and support, I extend a large "thank you" to the APICS professional staff.

Please send your comments about this publication to me at

APICS—The Educational Society for Resource Management
5301 Shawnee Road
Alexandria, Virginia 22312-2317

I look forward to your suggestions for future editions.

Elizabeth B. Davis

AUTHOR'S NOTE: Although the names, addresses, educational institutions, educational backgrounds, professional certifications, and job descriptions used as examples throughout this handbook may be inspired by real people, organizations, and institutions, all of the information is fictional.

TABLE OF CONTENTS

TABLE OF CONTENTS

1

SECTION 1:
PREPARING TO
MARKET YOURSELF

SECTION 1:
PREPARING TO MARKET YOURSELF

A job search is a marketing project. The product being marketed is You!

A job search is no different from any other task you manage. Consequently, project management tools may be used with great success throughout the job-search process.

As you begin your job search, take the time to establish your goal. What do you want to accomplish through this job search? A different job? A better job? What is "better"? Different responsibilities? More responsibility? Greater compensation? More control? More freedom?

In other words, answer the question,
"What do I want in a new job?"
in as much detail as possible.

Effective product marketing demands that you have a clear idea of how you meet the employer's needs.

Consequently, your next question should be,
"What do employers want?"

Quantify your value to the marketplace by documenting what you have to offer, being sure to document your on-the-job experience and your off-the-job experience gained through professional societies and other forms of volunteerism.

Finally, create a timeline for conducting your job search.

Unless you can dedicate more than one to two hours per day to your job search, your preparation will take six to seven weeks. Please note the word "preparation." Your preparation will become the foundation for your entire job search. This foundation will be strengthened by your commitment to (1) thorough, creative documentation and (2) a no-surprises administrative environment.

CREATIVE DOCUMENTATION

First, document what you are looking for in a new job and why.

Research the needs of the marketplace. If your background is not measuring up to the marketplace you want to enter, begin developing expertise through volunteerism or education.

Document your value to the marketplace. Begin by writing down your job responsibilities in an uncensored manner. Quantify each responsibility in time spent on each task. Describe each task—citing people supervised, revenue earned, costs contained or saved, and so forth.

Document each of these issues in writing. Whether you use index cards, word processing, or handwritten notes, it's important to put this information in a format that can be easily referenced throughout the job search.

Review your collection of kudos to discern how others viewed your past contributions. Was it your

> — ability to execute and implement a project plan?

> — success in integrating the needs of the entire enterprise?

> — superior supervisory skills?

> — ability to create and sustain a productive relationship with a vendor?

Create a chronological portfolio of your kudos that you can share with an interviewer on request.

Integrate your record of accomplishments with your knowledge of the marketplace and your value to the marketplace. This integration will be documented in your résumé and the correspondence used throughout your job search.

NO-SURPRISES ADMINISTRATION

Facing no surprises requires your attention to the administrative aspects of a job search. Use whatever tools work best for you.

The following checklist provides examples of tasks that support no-surprises administration:

— Call the registrar's office of each academic institution you attended and perform an over-the-phone background check on yourself. Because data entry errors occur, it's important for you to know how you are listed in the institution's database. Make a note of the phone number you used, the date and time you called, and the name of the person with whom you spoke. If your information does not match the registrar's, do all you can to resolve the matter before you send out your first résumé.

— Order a transcript from every academic institution you have attended.

— Contact professional societies. Find out their procedures for documenting your membership and/or certification. Ensure that your information matches theirs. Again, if your information does not match theirs, do all you can to resolve the matter before sending out your first résumé.

— Contact your references. Make sure you have the correct spelling of their names and titles, the names of employers, and the correct contact information (addresses, e-mail addresses, and phone numbers).

— Document your salary history. Make sure all dates and dollar amounts match those recorded with former employers. If you generated a substantial portion of your income through bonuses, commissions, or overtime, make copies of your W-2 forms.

— Have your résumé, business card, letterhead, and envelope professionally printed.

— Organize your work area.

— Set up a filing system for your job search. Make a folder for each informational interview requested and each response to an advertisement.

- Document the names and titles of anyone you know at a company.

- Document the gist of any phone calls you have with representatives of a company.

- Retain a copy of all of your correspondence to a company as well as its correspondence to you.

— Prepare your family. Talk about how their answering of phones, taking messages, and transmitting messages accurately can affect the success of your job search.

— Perform library or Web-based searches of the employers that interest you.

— Document all of the resources available to you:

- Friends

- Civic organizations

- Professional organizations, such as APICS

- Agencies specializing in recruitment and/or outplacement, such as APICS Career Services.

SAMPLE TIMELINE

The following sample timeline illustrates preparatory steps for a job search.

1. WEEK ONE

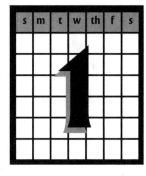

— Organize your work area.

— Set up your filing system to administer the job search process.

— Each day, document what you want in a new job and what you expect in a new employer.

— Each day, document your job responsibilities in an uncensored manner. Review job descriptions, kudos, performance appraisals, self-appraisals, and old résumés for measurements, industry-standard terms, descriptive phrases, and quantification.

— Each day, document meaningful off-the-job responsibilities. Has your work with civic organizations or professional societies, such as APICS, produced experience with project management, budget management, team facilitation, marketing, or training or contributed to a professional body of knowledge? Again, use measurements, industry-standard terms, and succinct, descriptive phrases.

— Compile a collection of your kudos.

— Call academic institutions and verify your educational achievements. Resolve differences. Order copies of transcripts.

— Call professional societies and verify your membership and any certifications you have earned. Resolve differences.

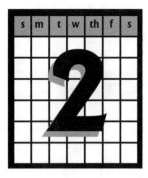

2. Week Two

— Review your on-the-job and off-the-job information. Ensure that all dates and measurements are accurate. Document skills that are transferable from job to job.

— Begin building an accurate salary history. Make copies of W-2 forms.

— Begin thinking about who should be your references.

— Call local printers and note what services they provide. Record the costs of printing résumés, letterhead, envelopes, and business cards.

— Compose a rough first draft of your résumé. Do not worry about formatting. Let it rest for a couple of days.

3. Week Three

— Call the persons you are considering as references. Have a conversation about their perceptions of your strengths and weaknesses. Discern their willingness to be professional references.

— Begin to refine the rough draft of your résumé. Start integrating your knowledge of the marketplace, your references' comments, and your background into this marketing piece. Target this brochure to your market's interests. Incorporate the whole you, not just the on-the-job you.

— Review and refine the résumé again.

— Show your draft résumé to someone who understands what you do and to someone else who does not understand your day-to-day responsibilities. Listen to the questions they ask, and integrate the answers into the next draft of your résumé.

— Decide whether a chronological résumé or a skill-based résumé markets you best. Decide what résumé format markets the product best.

— Review and refine the résumé.

4. WEEK FOUR

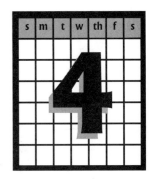

— Ensure that you have received any transcripts and/or verification of memberships and professional credentials; if not, follow up.

— Review and refine the résumé again. One more time: use industry-standard terminology, and ensure that all accomplishments are quantified.

— Use all proofreading resources available to you: friends, family, and automated spell-check devices. If grammar and spelling are not your strengths, let someone else perform these tasks for you.

— Review and refine your résumé one more time in the presence of others. If it is not yet the marketing brochure you want to use, review and refine it until it is.

— Have your résumé, letterhead, envelopes, and business cards professionally printed.

— Begin compiling the list of questions you expect to be asked. Begin formulating your answers.

— Compose a 30-second, self-introduction to use at career fairs, during stress interviews, and at professional society meetings.

5. WEEK FIVE

— Write to the persons who agreed to be your references and formally thank them. Provide them with information about what you want them to emphasize and a copy of the latest draft of your résumé.

— Finalize your salary history.

— Begin compiling a list of companies and/or individuals you will contact for informational interviews. Complete library and/or Web-based informational searches.

— Brief your family on phone procedures. If your family shares an e-mail address, brief them on how incoming e-mail should be read and saved.

— Ensure that all of the equipment to be used throughout the search—from phone to e-mail to printer—is in good working order.

— Purchase notepads to keep by the phone.

6. WEEK SIX

— Compose the list of questions you will ask of every interviewer.

— Set daily goals, such as the following:

– Request at least one informational interview; establish a date-tickler file to make sure you check the status of your request in a timely manner.

– Read one industry article and outline your thoughts and questions; discuss your thoughts and questions with a peer.

— Set weekly goals, such as the following:

– Respond to at least one advertisement.

– Follow up on requests for informational interviews.

– Share a meal with a friend who supports your job search.

– Role play an interview with a friend; use the questions you think you may be asked and the questions you want to ask.

— Set monthly goals, such as the following:

– Attend professional development seminars.

– Attend meetings of your membership society.

— Track all events.

SECTION 2:
MARKETING CHOICES

SECTION 2:
MARKETING CHOICES

YOUR RÉSUMÉ

Your résumé is a marketing brochure for a specific product: you. A résumé markets your assets to an industry, a company, or to a particular job. When done well, a résumé is the marketing brochure that persuades a company to interview an individual.

Your résumé should be a clear and concise marketing document. It should not exceed two pages in length. A bibliography of more than two citations should be printed separately and attached.

Including professional development activities and achievements, such as those available through APICS education and volunteerism, strengthens a résumé.

Like other marketing documents, the degree of success a résumé generates will be affected by how you have represented product quality, the strength and size of the list of potential users of the product, and the reputation of the product. Although it may take a while for you to think of yourself as a product, once you do, this perspective will help you to assess your employability in the marketplace more realistically.

During a job search, many variables are at work. The only variables you can control are the quality of the creative documents you submit, your personal presentation during the interview process, and the degree of commitment you have made to no-surprises administration.

Beware of providing truly personal information on a résumé or any document associated with a job search. If the information is not job-related, it could be used to your disadvantage during the job search, either subjectively or overtly. Therefore, omit references to pastimes, marital status, political affiliation, parental status, and so forth. Remember that the space available on your marketing brochure is limited. Use the space available for information that applies to your job search.

Age discrimination exists. References to more than 20 years of experience should be considered very carefully. Describing 15 to 20 years of experience on a résumé is sufficient. The purpose of the résumé is to ensure that you are invited for an interview; it's not a biography.

When using abbreviations, such as MRP, MRP II, and ERP, make sure they are industry-standard, not company-standard, abbreviations. The acronyms of specific software packages must be presented accurately.

Use all references available to you for proofreading your résumé and collateral job-search materials. Software tools are great! However, always proofread for content as well as spelling and grammar. If the position you seek requires attention to detail and your résumé contains spelling and grammar errors or you haven't signed your cover letter, you may lessen your chances of being interviewed.

When choosing a format, font, and type size for your résumé, your choice reflects your style. Clarity, consistency, and a professional image should be your goals.

TYPES OF RÉSUMÉS

In general terms, a résumé will either be skill-based or chronological. No rules apply! Choose the résumé type that best markets you to your audience.

The heart of a skill-based résumé is a grouping of professional skills. A skill-based résumé documents your expertise in skills that are transferable from job to job and from industry to industry. Individuals with many years of experience who want to avoid repeating the same job responsibilities from job to job may choose to represent those responsibilities by grouping them together. A skill-based résumé may also be helpful to someone who does not want to draw attention to time gaps in employment because of downsizing, illness, reentry into the job market, or a change in career focus.

A chronological résumé, on the other hand, provides a chronological review of current experience, followed by past experience. Individuals with a progressively responsible work history should consider the benefits of a chronological résumé.

SKILL-BASED RÉSUMÉ

A skill-based résumé consists of the following parts:

Part 1: Name, credentials, contact information (e.g., address, e-mail address, home phone number)

Part 2: Professional summary

Part 3: Overview of key skills and achievements

Part 4: Brief work chronology (e.g., title, company, dates of employment)

Part 5: Academic achievements, meaningful training, and documentation of professional credentials

Part 6: Documentation of volunteerism or professional memberships

Part 7: Bibliography, when applicable.

CHRONOLOGICAL RÉSUMÉ

A chronological résumé consists of the following parts:

Part 1: Name, credentials, contact information (e.g., address, e-mail address, home phone number)

Part 2: Professional summary

Part 3: Chronological work history, beginning with information about your most recent job and working backward 20 years

Part 4: Academic achievements, meaningful training, and documentation of professional credentials

Part 5: Documentation of volunteerism or professional memberships

Part 6: Bibliography, when applicable.

PRESENT YOUR NAME, CREDENTIALS, AND CONTACT INFORMATION

You may present your name formally or informally. For example, I have the option of referring to myself as "Elizabeth" (my legal name) or "Betsy," (which is how I'm known). How you want to be known is up to you.

If you have earned credentials, such as CFPIM, CPIM, or CIRM, present that information appropriately after your name in the first part of the résumé (example: John Doe, CFPIM, CPIM, CIRM). Many jobs require APICS certification. Ensure that the reader knows your qualifications quickly. In other words, don't save this information for the end of your résumé.

Think about how you want to be contacted and about what processes you will set in motion. For example, if you put your work phone number or company e-mail address on your résumé, will you be able to respond with privacy? After all, most employers tell employees not to expect privacy when using company resources. Is this how you want your employer to learn of your job search?

Do you want to send the message to a potential employer that you are using your current employer's resources to conduct your job search and that you are conducting your job search on that employer's time? I've often wondered if an applicant who uses an employer's fax machine to fax résumés realizes that the employer's name is stamped on the résumés.

If you include an e-mail address on your résumé, make sure you check your e-mail regularly.

However you choose to present your name, credentials, and contact information, present it accurately. Make sure this information is consistent throughout all of your documents, from résumé to letterhead to business card to envelope.

Be wary of using boxes or other graphics unless you have the design expertise to use graphics effectively. Looking "boxed in" may not draw positive attention.

Sample formats for presenting your name, credentials, and contact information follow.

Sample 1: Centered, boldface, and in a slightly larger font
than the rest of the résumé

REGINALD X. CAPUTO, C.P.M., CPIM
444 Job Lookers' Drive, Bowling Green, KY 43434
phone: (332) 555-1212   e-mail: RXCap@looking.com

Sample 2: Justified, boldface, and with the name in a slightly larger font
than the rest of the résumé

Reginald Caputo, CFPIM, CIRM_____

444 Job Lookers' Drive, Bowling Green, KY 43434
phone: (332) 555-1212   e-mail: RXCap@looking.com

Sample 3: Information communicated in a centered header and footer

Reginald X. Caputo, Ph.D., CFPIM, CIRM

<résumé text>

444 Job Lookers' Drive, Bowling Green, KY 43434
phone: (332) 555-1212   e-mail: RXCap@looking.com

Sample 4: Right-justified information

Reginald X. Caputo, CPA, CIRM

444 Job Lookers' Drive, Bowling Green, KY 43434
phone: (332) 555-1212
e-mail: RXCap@looking.com

Sample 5: Left-justified information

Reginald X. Caputo, CIRM, CIWA, Jonah

444 Job Lookers' Drive, Bowling Green, KY 43434
phone: (332) 555-1212 e-mail: RXCap@looking.com

17

SUMMARIZE YOUR PROFESSION

More than one book on résumé composition suggests leading your résumé with an objective. This is not one of those books.

An objective describes what you want out of the job-search process. Expressing your wishes is not marketing the product. Consequently, it adds no value and wastes precious marketing space. A résumé is not the place to express personal desires.

However, a résumé is the place to tell a recruiter why an interview is appropriate. A professional summary of 5 to 10 lines that describes your key assets is an excellent way of communicating why you meet the recruiter's needs. A recruiter may be reviewing upward of 100 résumés at a time. Tell the recruiter up front in the résumé everything that is important about you. Use industry-standard terminology instead of jargon.

The following examples show professional summaries.

EXAMPLE 1

Manufacturing professional whose leadership, adherence to best practices, and commitment to lifelong professional education has supported quality work processes in a world-class manufacturing environment. Strategic goal achiever. Experience is concentrated in materials management, production support services, quality control, and safety. Possess particular expertise in sales and operations planning, shop-floor management, purchasing, and production and inventory management. Experienced staff supervisor and team leader. APICS-qualified instructor in production and inventory management.

EXAMPLE 2

Materials manager whose 10 years of industry experience have been concentrated in plant environments. Possess progressively responsible track record that demonstrates solid results in business growth, cost reductions, and improvements in inventory turns and customer satisfaction levels. Enthusiastic user of TQM and JIT principles. Efficient user of ERP, spreadsheets, and word-processing packages. College graduate. APICS-certified in Production and Inventory Management (CPIM) and Integrated Resource Management (CIRM). Experienced trainer in on-the-job and formal seminar situations.

EXAMPLE 3

Manufacturing professional whose progressively responsible industry experience has been concentrated in purchasing and materials management. Possess CPIM and C.P.M. professional credentials. Experienced planner and implementer of ERP technology. Skilled team leader, staff supervisor, and trainer in supply chain management. Possess TOP SECRET clearance. Efficient user of automated manufacturing systems and off-the-shelf office technology. Fluent in Spanish and English; conversant in Portuguese and French.

EXAMPLE 4

Purchasing professional whose five years of experience have been concentrated in the power industry. Experience demonstrates commitment to best practices and impressive results in purchasing, cost containment, process improvement, and quality analysis. Skilled ISO 9000 team leader. Supervise six direct reports and two 30-person, cross-functional work teams. Contributed significantly to implementation of MRP. College graduate. Certified Purchasing Manager. Pursuing CPIM certification.

EXAMPLE 5

Manufacturing professional whose three years of experience have been concentrated in quality assurance and safety in a plant environment. Have gained significant exposure to materials management and purchasing management. Contributed to process improvement team that led to implementation of JIT and ERP. Computer-literate college graduate. Possess academic knowledge and on-the-job experience with supply chain management and constraints management.

USE MEASUREMENTS

Whether you've decided to use a skill-based résumé or a chronological résumé, how you document your achievements must reflect a strong understanding of the strategic importance of your job. One of the best ways to provide this type of information is by using measurements throughout your résumé. In addition to providing depth to the experience described, using measurements indicates an awareness that measurements run successful businesses.

The more measurements you provide in your résumé, the more likely you will be perceived as an individual who gets things done. Using measurements shows you are a person who "accomplishes goals" rather than one who "has responsibilities."

Review your preparatory work on documenting your current and past responsibilities and achievements as well as your significant off-the-job achievements. Then, quantify, quantify, quantify! Every professional person has responsibilities. Your résumé must describe what you have done and how you have done it. Throughout the text, use action words that describe accomplishments, level of decision-making authority, job environments, and teams and individuals; quantify these accomplishments in terms of people supervised, dollars, square footage, production, quality improvements, inventory turns, and so forth.

Which of the following two descriptions describes what an employer needs to know?

Have responsibility for budget oversight.

or

Have planning and oversight authority for a $500,000 product budget, a $250,000 salary budget, and a $150,000 discretionary bonus budget. Use Excel spreadsheet technology to produce monthly reports and adjust quarterly forecasts.

Use Powerful Descriptors

Accomplishment-based words and phrases should be used as often and as accurately as possible. A brief list follows.

LIST OF POWERFUL DESCRIPTORS

Accomplish	Goal Achiever
Achieve	Goal-directed
Accountable	Goal Management
Administer	Goal Orientation
Analyze	Implement
Authorize	Improve
Change Manager	Increase
Change Planner	Led/Leadership
Debug	Manage
Decisionmaker	Negotiate
Design	Plan
Develop	Resource Planner
Distribute	Strategic Planner
Edit	Supervise
Empower	Team Builder
Enterprise	Team Contributor
Execute	Team Facilitator
Facilitate	Team Leader

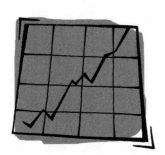

The following are examples of how to quantify accomplishments:

— Member of a leadership team that grew the business from $10 million to $31 million in three years while reducing overhead expenses by 13 percent.

— Analyzed opportunities for cost reductions and realized a $247,000 cost reduction in one fiscal period.

— Planned and implemented JIT and achieved a 30 percent inventory reduction and a 200 percent increase in inventory turns.

— Improved inventory accuracy from 79 percent to 99.5 percent in six months.

— Raised supplier quality-assurance ratings from 90 percent to 99.99 percent in one year.

— Led a 14-person work group comprising exempt and non-exempt staff.

— Negotiated the purchase of all materials; produced $101,000 in annual cost savings.

— Used value-analysis techniques to improve purchasing processes and eliminate redundant processes.

— Managed a $6 million inventory with 880 discrete products.

— Used change-management techniques during a TQM implementation.

— Oversaw the planning, layout, and move of a 60,000-square-foot warehouse to a new facility.

— Improved supplier and on-time deliveries from 80 percent to 95 percent in one fiscal period.

— Reduced available-to-promise inventory by 75 percent.

— Designed and implemented a product quality improvement program; identified root causes of problems through continuous statistical measurements and analyses.

— Developed and implemented a customer-rating program to gauge product satisfaction; used phone interviews, site visits, and reply cards. Response increased from 1.5 percent to 9 percent over prior rating program.

— Developed and implemented in-house educational programs that support industry best practices. Staff productivity increased 29 percent immediately after training and has been sustained at a 25 percent increase over a 12-month period.

— Developed safety orientation program. Achieved 100 percent OSHA compliance. Reduced time lost to accidents by 75 percent in a six-month period. Improved attendance by 23 percent and decreased accident-related costs by 150 percent. Reduced involuntary staff attrition by 16 percent in one year.

— Successfully initiated performance measurements for a 20-person materials management staff. Within one year, goal achievement rose from 42 percent to 89 percent.

— Worked with corporate human resources in establishing career paths for a 20-person materials management staff.

— Planned and oversaw the implementation of ISO 9001, ERP, and MRP II; each was accomplished on time and within budget.

— Used goal setting and motivational techniques in supervising staff; experienced the lowest turnover rate (7 percent) and highest job satisfaction rating (92 percent) of any supervisor.

GROUP YOUR SKILLS IN A SKILL-BASED RÉSUMÉ

If you've decided to use a skill-based résumé, review your preparatory work on documenting your current and past responsibilities and achievements as well as your significant off-the-job achievements.

Group them into skill areas and then decide where each of your accomplishments should be listed.

The following examples of skill areas and descriptions are provided to stimulate some "out-of-the-box" thinking on your part about how to describe and market yourself.

MANUFACTURING INNOVATION

❏ Researched, analyzed, recommended, and implemented external supplier stocking, restocking, and point-of-use delivery program. Initiated use of Just-in-Time for raw materials and components. Improved supplier on-time deliveries from 80 percent to 95 percent in one year.

❏ Researched, analyzed, recommended, and implemented shop-floor improvements. Used dispatch rules and moved toward a pull production system. Improved on-time shipments from 50 percent to 95 percent in six months.

PROCESS IMPROVEMENTS

❏ Led a process improvement team whose research and analysis resulted in a 300 percent increase in business revenues over three years, $250,000 in annual cost reductions, a 30 percent reduction in inventory, and a 200 percent increase in inventory turns. Improved inventory accuracy from 79 percent to 99 percent in one year.

SUPERVISION OF TEAMS AND STAFF

❏ Supervise a 10-person materials management staff. Facilitate a 15-person, cross-functional product review team whose functions include materials, production, inventory, purchasing, pricing, sales, and marketing professionals. Interview, make hiring recommendations, and conduct performance appraisals twice annually. Ensure that orientation and on-the-job training support philosophies of TQM, personal accountability, empowerment, and goal achievement. Lowest level of staff attrition of any supervisor.

❏ Chair a 20-person committee oriented to continuous improvement of the professional credential, Certified in Production and Inventory Management (CPIM). Use leadership skills and knowledge of the APICS body of knowledge to facilitate teleconferences and meetings. Work collaboratively with APICS professional staff in accomplishing objectives. Review $2 million budget annually.

TRAINING AND DEVELOPMENT

❏ Qualified instructor in the APICS professional body of knowledge for production and inventory management and the basics of supply chain management. Trained groups ranging in size from 5 to 50 in seminar and on-the-job environments.

❏ Qualified instructor in constraints management. Marketed, negotiated, and executed in-house training programs in corporate settings for groups of 10 to 50.

EDUCATIONAL BEST PRACTICES

❏ Developed and supported in-house education programs supporting best practices. Implemented, supported, and expanded product-oriented Quick Ship Programs. Significantly enhanced staff employability in a competitive marketplace.

❏ Developed and delivered education and training programs on safety and environmental issues. Documented best practices and personally provided training to facilities managers, frontline supervisors, and plant personnel. Achieved 100 percent OSHA compliance. Reduced time lost to injuries and accidents by 75 percent. Decreased accident-related costs by 440 percent over three years.

DISTRIBUTION MANAGEMENT

❏ Manage a $5 million inventory for a catalog sales operation that completes 10 inventory turns annually with 98 percent warehouse accuracy. Eighty percent of all orders are shipped on the day of order. Almost 100 percent of all orders are shipped within 24 hours of order.

CALL CENTER MANAGEMENT

❏ Manage a 20-person, inbound call center that processes 22,000 calls monthly with an on-phone ratio of 73 percent and a 96 percent customer-satisfaction rating.

❏ Manage a 10-person, outbound telemarketing sales center that generates $15 million in annual revenue.

WAREHOUSE MANAGEMENT

❏ Direct the operations of a 120,000-square-foot warehouse that operates 24 hours, 7 days a week.

❏ Supervise a 20-person, full- and part-time distribution staff.

❏ Generated $600,000 in cost savings through lease renegotiations.

DOCUMENT YOUR WORK HISTORY IN A SKILL-BASED RÉSUMÉ

If you are using a skill-based résumé, a chronological bare-bones work history should follow your skills. Make it short and to the point: Title, Dates, Company Name, Company Location. Samples of how to present this information and a sample skill-based résumé follow.

SAMPLE 1 OF A SKILL-BASED RÉSUMÉ

WORK HISTORY

Consultant to the Manufacturing Work Group, Big 4 Accounting Firm (Nashville, TN), June 1997–present.

Materials Manager, The Best Company in the World (Bestown, KY), February 1992–May 1997.

Purchasing Manager, The Best Company in the World (Jackson, TN), February 1990–January 1992.

Purchasing Agent, The Best Company in the World (Jackson, TN), June 1988–January 1990.

SAMPLE 2 OF A SKILL-BASED RÉSUMÉ

WORK HISTORY

Big Four Accounting Firm	Nashville, TN
Consultant, Manufacturing Work Group	1997–present
The Best Company in the World	Bestown, KY
Materials Manager	1992–1997
Purchasing Manager	1990–1992
Purchasing Agent	1988–1990

DOCUMENT YOUR ACHIEVEMENTS IN A CHRONOLOGICAL RÉSUMÉ

If, after completing your preparatory work, you decide a chronological résumé works best for you, begin with your most recent job and work your way back no more than 15 to 20 years. Concentrate on achievements and true measurements. Avoid anecdotal evidence. Include your title, the timeframe the title was active, the company name, and the location of your office (city/state). A sample follows.

CHRONOLOGY OF WORK ACHIEVEMENTS

Big Four Consulting Company   Jackson, TN
Consultant, Manufacturing Work Group   June 1997–present

Created the manufacturing work group to respond to process reengineering and professional service needs of national client base. Analyze opportunities for revenue growth, cost reduction, and process improvement. Respond to requests for information and requests for proposals. Generated $500,000 in revenue in 1997 and $1.5 million in revenue in 1998. Personally provide training and develop on-the-job training programs for client companies in supply chain management, Just-in-Time (JIT), and capacity planning. Post-training productivity improvements for JIT and capacity rose from 36 percent to 60 percent immediately following training and reached 72 percent six months after training. Post-training productivity improvements for supply chain management rose from 51 percent to 92 percent immediately following training and reached 95 percent six months after training.

The Best Company in the World   Bestown, KY
Materials Manager   February 1992–May 1997
Purchasing Manager   March 1990–January 1992
Purchasing Agent   June 1988–February 1990

Successfully planned and implemented material handling techniques to improve business processes. Purchased copper, steel plate, steel sheets, and fasteners. Oversaw purchasing for maintenance, repair, and operations (MRO) supplies as well as stores operations. Used change management techniques during TQM implementation. Oversaw implementation of ISO 9001, MPS, and MRP. Measured accomplishments include the following:

— Facilitated a process review team whose implemented ideas generated a 300 percent increase in revenue over three years, resulted in annual reduced costs of $250,000, and produced a 30 percent inventory reduction

— Improved inventory accuracy from 79 percent to 99.5 percent within six months

— Improved inventory turns by 200 percent over one year

— Improved customer on-time rating from 70 percent to 95 percent over one year.

— Improved customer quality-assurance ratings from 90 percent to 99.9 percent over one year.

DOCUMENT YOUR EDUCATION AND PROFESSIONAL CREDENTIALS

Whether you are using a chronological résumé or a skill-based résumé, this section generally appears toward the end of the résumé. Again, be accurate and straightforward. Providing the year the degree/credential was earned is up to you.

When documenting professional credentials, use the word "certified" very carefully. Receiving a certificate is not the same as being certified. Consequently, if you have passed one or more of the CPIM or CIRM modules but are not yet certified, don't use the word "certified." It would be more accurate to say, "Successfully completed." Samples follow.

SAMPLE 1 OF ACADEMIC AND PROFESSIONAL CREDENTIALS

ACADEMIC AND PROFESSIONAL CREDENTIALS

Pursuing Master of Business Administration degree, George Washington University Executive Program (Washington, DC); June 2000 graduation anticipated.

Certified in Production and Inventory Management (CPIM), conferred by APICS, 1994.

Certified Purchasing Manager (C.P.M.), conferred by the National Association of Purchasing Management, 1992.

Bachelor of Science degree, Manufacturing Sciences, LeHigh University (LeHigh, OH), December 1987. Graduated magna cum laude.

SAMPLE 2 OF ACADEMIC AND PROFESSIONAL CREDENTIALS

ACADEMIC AND PROFESSIONAL CREDENTIALS

Pursuing Associate of Science degree in Business Management, Northern Virginia Community College (Annandale); June 1999 graduation anticipated.

Successfully completed three of the modules necessary for eventual Certified in Production and Inventory Management (CPIM) status; on track to complete all modules by December 1999. ·

Successfully completed coursework in accounting (12 hours), business law (6 hours), and logistics (3 hours) at Prince George's County Community College (Largo, MD), 1988–89.

DESCRIBE YOUR VOLUNTEER ACTIVITIES

In the course of completing your preparatory work, do not overlook experience you have gained as a volunteer. Significant volunteer activities through APICS and other professional societies have probably exposed you to a level of business acumen not commonly possessed by individuals in your profession.

APICS volunteers typically possess decision-making authority, public speaking experience, and fiscal oversight responsibility at the national, regional, or chapter level. Many gain knowledge and hands-on experience in leadership, enterprise management, team building and facilitation, marketing, communications, meetings management, and product research and development. Chapter officers manage independently incorporated, not-for-profit organizations and must be attuned to all the legal and financial responsibilities such an entity requires. Committee members may have tremendous impact on courseware and education, member recruitment and retention, and the financial health of the Society.

Put yourself in an employer's position. If you could choose between two materials managers who have identical experience and academic background, but one is CPIM certified and is an APICS-qualified instructor in production and inventory management and the other is not, which would be your first choice? APICS volunteer activities strengthen your résumé!

Although I do not recommend providing personal information on a résumé, volunteer experience gained on behalf of a church, synagogue, or other faith center can be appropriate when presented in a business-oriented manner.

Descriptions of skills and accomplishments associated with volunteer activities are no different from descriptions of skills and accomplishments associated with a job. Measurements and accomplishment-based descriptions should be used. The following sample volunteer descriptions show how volunteer activities might be described.

VOLUNTEER ACTIVITY SAMPLES

1998 to 1999—President, Jaycees of Bestown, Kentucky. Popularly elected to manage this 500-person chapter that successfully raised $167,000—a record high—for charity in 1998. Collaborated with other elected officers in redesigning communication tools and selecting prominent speakers. Increased membership by 17 percent in one year and held member attrition to 5 percent.

1993 to present—Mentor to the Student Chapter, Future Business Leaders of America. Counsel 100-student high school chapter on business trends, with special emphasis on the manufacturing and service industries. Provide public-speaking engagements quarterly. Develop and present PowerPoint presentations. Serve as a professional mentor to two students per semester.

1995 to 1999—Trustee, First Baptist Church. One of 12 stewards elected to manage the financial operations of this $6 million per year, not-for-profit enterprise serving 5,000 members. Analyzed, designed, implemented, and improved business operating processes. Reduced expenses by 15 percent in one year. Spearheaded image campaign that included creating a Web site, running a direct-mail marketing campaign, and increasing funding of outreach ministries.

1988 to present—Volunteer, Bestown Literacy Program. Teach two adults to read each year.

APICS Board of Directors. Currently serve as a member of the elected 23-person, board of directors of APICS, a $29 million per year professional society dedicated to individual and organizational education, standards of excellence, and information in integrated resource management. Through service on the Membership and Chapter Development Committee, share fiscal and strategic planning responsibilities for the APICS organization's 72,000 members, 250,000 customers, 270 chapters, and 120 staff members.

APICS Region Staff. Appointed to provide volunteer assistance to an elected Region Vice President in meeting educational and certification goals by APICS chapters in this 3-state, 20-chapter region. Visit chapters. Successfully completed volunteer leadership workshops in marketing and membership retention. Membership retention is up 21 percent; new corporate memberships are up 26 percent; new individual memberships have risen 12 percent.

APICS Emissary. Use business acumen and industry knowledge to establish relationships with local businesses and to provide information about the educational products and services available through the local chapter of

APICS and through the APICS organization. Work collaboratively with local training directors, human resources directors, and plant managers in designing on-site, educational programs.

APICS-qualified Instructor. Qualified by APICS as knowledgeable in the body of knowledge of production and inventory management and *Train the Trainer*. Have instructed workshops ranging in size from 5 to 50 manufacturing professionals.

APICS Chapter President. Serve as president of a local, 500-member chapter of APICS, an international educational society that provides products and services in production and inventory management and integrated resource management. Chapter size increased 20 percent during tenure.

Certified Fellow, Production and Inventory Management. Successfully earned the Certified in Production and Inventory Management (CPIM) credential. Named a "Certified Fellow" for my individual contributions to the P&IM body of knowledge.

Successfully completed the Basics of Supply Chain Management, the first educational credential leading to CPIM certification (1999).

Certified in Production and Inventory Management (CPIM) in 1994; recertification expected in 1999.

Certified in Integrated Resource Management (CIRM) in 1997.

APICS Conference Committee Member. Member of the 1998 committee governing the APICS 41st International Conference and Exposition, which produced 200 educational opportunities over a four-day period, an 11,000-square-foot bookstore, a 1,500-vendor exhibit hall, and 3,500 paid attendees. (1996–1998)

Participant, Item-writing Workshops. Participated in developing new questions and answers for the certification examinations in the production and inventory management body of knowledge.

Contributor, *APICS—The Performance Advantage,* the monthly integrated resource management magazine. Author of articles on production and inventory management. (See attached bibliography.)

Public Speaker and Educator in the body of knowledge of integrated resource management to audiences of 50 to 100 persons. Most recent session: *Planning and Executing an ERP Implementation.*

Reginald Caputo, CFPIM, CIRM_____

444 Job Lookers' Drive, Bowling Green, KY 43434

phone: (332) 555-1212   e-mail: RXCap@looking.com

PROFESSIONAL OVERVIEW

Manufacturing professional whose leadership, adherence to best practices, and commitment to lifelong professional education support quality work processes in a world-class manufacturing environment. Strategic goal achiever. Experience is concentrated in materials management, production support services, quality control, and safety. Possess particular expertise in sales and operations planning, shop-floor management, purchasing, and production and inventory management. Experienced staff supervisor and team leader. APICS-qualified instructor in production and inventory management. Conversant in Spanish.

AREAS OF ACHIEVEMENT AND EXPERTISE

MANUFACTURING INNOVATION

❐ Researched, analyzed, recommended, and implemented External Supplier Stocking, Restocking, and Point-of-Use Delivery Program. Initiated use of Just-in-Time for raw materials and components. Improved supplier on-time deliveries from 80 percent to 95 percent in one year.

❐ Researched, analyzed, recommended, and implemented shop-floor improvements. Used dispatch rules; moved toward a pull production system. Improved on-time shipments from 50 percent to 95 percent in six months.

PROCESS IMPROVEMENTS

❐ Led a bilingual process improvement team whose research and analysis resulted in a 300 percent increase in business revenues over three years, $1.2 million in annual cost reductions, a 30 percent reduction in inventory, a 200 percent increase in inventory turns, and improved inventory accuracy from 79 percent to 99 percent in one year.

STAFF AND TEAM SUPERVISION

❐ Supervise a 10-person materials management staff. Facilitate a 15-person, cross-functional product review team comprising materials, production, inventory, purchasing, pricing, sales, and marketing professionals. Interview, make hiring recommendations, and conduct performance appraisals twice annually. Ensure orientation and on-the-job training supports philosophies of TQM, personal accountability, empowerment, and goal achievement.

TRAINING AND STAFF DEVELOPMENT

❏ Qualified instructor in supply chain management. Have trained groups ranging in size from 5 to 50 in seminar and on-the-job environments.

❏ Developed and delivered education and training programs for safety and environmental issues. Achieved 100 percent OSHA compliance. Reduced time lost to injuries and accidents by 75 percent. Decreased accident-related costs by 440 percent over three years.

WORK HISTORY

Consultant to the Manufacturing Work Group, Big 4 Accounting Firm (Nashville, TN), June 1997–present.

Materials Manager, The Best Company in the World (Bestown, KY), February 1992–May 1997.

Purchasing Manager, The Best Company in the World (Jackson, TN), February 1990–January 1992.

Purchasing Agent, The Best Company in the World (Jackson, TN), June 1988–January 1990.

ACADEMIC AND PROFESSIONAL CREDENTIALS

Bachelor of Science, Economics, University of Kansas (Lawrence), 1988.

Certified in Production and Inventory Management (CPIM), conferred by APICS, 1994; recertified 1999.

Certified in Integrated Resource Management (CIRM), conferred by APICS, 1996.

VOLUNTEERISM

1998–Present, APICS Emissary. Use business acumen and industry knowledge to establish relationships with local businesses and to provide information about the educational products and services available through the local chapter of APICS and through the APICS organization. Work collaboratively with local training directors, human resources directors, and plant managers in designing on-site, educational programs.

1994–Present, Instructor. Teach "Basics of Supply Chain Management" to groups of 20 to 100 manufacturing and service professionals.

Reginald Caputo, CFPIM, CIRM_____

444 Job Lookers' Drive, Bowling Green, KY 43434
phone: (332) 555-1212   e-mail: RXCap@looking.com

PROFESSIONAL OVERVIEW

Manufacturing professional whose leadership, adherence to best practices, and commitment to lifelong professional education support quality work processes in a world-class manufacturing environment. Strategic goal achiever. Experience is concentrated in materials management, production support services, quality control, and safety. Possess particular expertise in sales and operations planning, shop-floor management, purchasing, and production and inventory management. Experienced staff supervisor and team leader. APICS-qualified instructor in production and inventory management.

WORK HISTORY

Big Four Consulting Company   Jackson, TN
Consultant, Manufacturing Work Group   June 1997–present
Created the manufacturing work group to respond to process reengineering and professional service needs of national client base. Analyze opportunities for revenue growth, cost reduction, and process improvement. Respond to requests for information and requests for proposals. Generated $500,000 in revenue in 1997 and $1.5 million in revenue in 1998. Personally provide training and develop on-the-job training programs for client companies in supply chain management, Just-in-Time (JIT), and capacity planning. Post-training productivity improvements for JIT and capacity rose from 36 percent to 60 percent immediately following training and reached 72 percent six months after training. Post-training productivity improvements for supply chain management rose from 51 percent to 92 percent six months after training.

The Best Company in the World   Bestown, KY
Materials Manager   February 1992–May 1997
Purchasing Manager   March 1990–January 1992
Purchasing Agent   June 1988–February 1990

Successfully planned and implemented material handling techniques to improve business processes. Purchased copper, steel plate, steel sheets, and fasteners. Oversaw purchasing for maintenance, repair, and operations (MRO) supplies as well as stores operations. Used change management techniques during TQM implementation. Oversaw implementation of ISO 9001, MPS, and MRP. Measured accomplishments include the following:

— Facilitated a process review team whose implemented ideas generated a 300 percent increase in revenue over three years, resulted in annual reduced costs of $250,000, and produced a 30 percent inventory reduction.

— Improved inventory accuracy from 79 percent to 99.5 percent within six months.

— Improved inventory turns 200 percent over one year.

— Improved customer on-time rating from 70 percent to 95 percent over one year.

— Improved customer quality-assurance ratings from 90 percent to 99.9 percent over one year.

ACADEMIC AND PROFESSIONAL CREDENTIALS

Bachelor of Science, Economics, University of Kansas (Lawrence), 1988.

Certified in Production and Inventory Management (CPIM), conferred by APICS, 1994; recertified 1999.

Certified in Integrated Resource Management (CIRM), conferred by APICS, 1996.

VOLUNTEERISM

<u>1998 to Present, APICS Emissary</u>. Use business acumen and industry knowledge to establish relationships with local businesses and provide information about the educational products and services available through the local chapter of APICS, and through the APICS organization. Work collaboratively with local training directors, human resources directors, and plant managers in designing on-site educational programs.

<u>1995 to 1998, Trustee, First Baptist Church</u>. One of 12 stewards elected to manage the operations of this $6 million/year not-for-profit enterprise serving 5,000 members. Improved business processes. Implemented a Web site image campaign and a direct-mail marketing campaign. New members increased 25 percent in one year.

SECTION 3:
HOW YOUR REFERENCES
MARKET YOU

SECTION 3:
HOW YOUR REFERENCES MARKET YOU

Your references market you through their knowledge of your experience, your accomplishments, and your value to the marketplace. Consequently, your choice of references is important.

Use your references, first, to discern what they perceive as your chief assets. Incorporate their thoughts into your résumé.

Make sure you have the reference's permission before submitting his or her name. Take the time to discuss which areas you want your reference to particularly highlight (see page 5-6, "Sample Letter to Send to a Reference").

Unless it's specifically requested, do not provide a list of references with your résumé. It's not necessary to write "references upon request." Recruiters assume you will have references.

However, always make sure you have the name, title, company name, and contact information for every reference before an interview. Take that information with you to the interview. Your preparation is key; by ensuring that your reference contact information is accurate, you have helped to ensure the smooth course of any background check.

Unless specifically requested, avoid using personal references. However, if you must provide them, choose individuals who have some knowledge of your values and your accomplishments.

Some people find it helpful to compile the letters of reference and kudos earned during their careers into a portfolio. This portfolio may be presented at an appropriate time to an interviewer. However, because most companies face stringent reference-checking requirements, do not be disappointed if the interviewer does not take this information at face value.

The following is a sample list of references and the information needed for each.

SAMPLE LIST OF REFERENCES

Reginald X. Caputo, Ph.D., CFPIM, CIRM

444 JOB LOOKERS' DRIVE, BOWLING GREEN, KY 43434
PHONE: (332) 555-1212   E-MAIL: RXCAP@LOOKING.COM

PROFESSIONAL REFERENCE	DESCRIPTION
Warren Boss Happy Landings, Inc. 11 Yellow Brick Road Ozville, KY 44232 (332) 555-1212, ext. 4545	Supervisor, 1997–present
Langdon Colquitter Happy Landings, Inc. 11 Yellow Brick Road Ozville, KY 44232 (332) 555-1212, ext. 4234	Member of the bilingual, cross-functional ERP implementation team I led from 1996–1998.
Lawrence G. Knowledge, Ph.D. 1600 Pennsylvania Avenue Washington, DC 20037 (800) 999-5555, ext. 1231	ERP vendor I worked with from 1997–1998.

PERSONAL REFERENCE	DESCRIPTION
Joani Teacherton Purchasing Manager Alloys Are U.S., Inc. Cincinnati, OH 44231 (800) 222-2222, ext. 2323	President of the local APICS chapter; I provided education in supply chain management and in *Train the Trainer* for her chapter.

SECTION 4:
YOUR SALARY HISTORY

SECTION 4:
YOUR SALARY HISTORY

When a salary history is requested in a job advertisement, the recruiter is usually trying to find out the salary you are seeking.

Consequently, I do not recommend providing a salary history, because it consists of too much personal information and, after all, you don't know with certainty who is going to be reading your résumé. A salary history may be provided at the time of an interview.

Communicate your salary requirement accurately and concisely:

> "In my next position, I am seeking a starting annual salary of $60,000."

> "My current salary is in the mid-sixties, and I am seeking a starting annual salary of $70,000."

Communicate your reservations in a professional manner:

> "If selected for an interview, I will be happy to provide a salary history at that time."

When compiling your salary history, be aware that it should reflect only compensation earned by salary, wages, bonuses, commissions, or other monetary awards. It should not include the dollar amount your employer spends on benefits such as insurance.

You will be expected to produce historical salary information at the time of an interview. An application must be 100 percent accurate. Any omissions or misrepresentations will, in general, result in your being dropped from the process. If bonuses or commissions or overtime have contributed greatly to your total compensation, your potential employer may ask to see your W-2 form for the period in question.

Samples of how to maintain historical salary information follow.

SAMPLE 1 OF A SALARY HISTORY

Reginald X. Caputo, CIRM, CIWA, Jonah

444 Job Lookers' Drive, Bowling Green, KY 43434
phone: (332) 555-1212 e-mail: RXCap@looking.com

SALARY HISTORY

AMOUNT	EVENT DESCRIPTION	EFFECTIVE DATE
$60,000	Annual salary	01-01-99
$57,400	Annual salary	01-01-98
$52,500	Starting salary at new job	01-05-97
$42,000	Salary at termination	12-15-96
$42,000	Annual salary	01-01-96
$38,500	Annual salary	01-01-95
$35,000	Annual salary	01-01-94

BONUS HISTORY

AMOUNT	EVENT DESCRIPTION	DATE OF AWARD
$5,000	Production bonus	12-31-98
$7,500	Production bonus	07-01-98
$2,500	Production bonus	04-01-98
$1,000	Achievement bonus (CIRM)	01-05-98
$3,000	Production bonus	12-31-98
$1,000	Production bonus	04-01-97
$1,000	Achievement bonus (CPIM)	03-31-96

Reginald X. Caputo, CPIM

444 Job Lookers' Drive, Bowling Green, KY 43434

phone: (332) 555-1212

e-mail: RXCap@looking.com

SALARY HISTORY

YEAR	HOURLY RATE/SALARY	TOTAL: WAGES+OVERTIME+BONUSES
1998	$29.26 ($60,860)	$72,222
1997	$27.02 ($56,201)	$58,315
1996	$25.00 ($52,000)	$67,444
1995	$23.90 ($49,712)	$55,433
1994	$22.02 ($45,801)	$60,988

SECTION 5:
YOUR CORRESPONDENCE

SECTION 5:
YOUR CORRESPONDENCE

The correspondence you generate during a job search speaks volumes about your character. Consequently, this correspondence serves as a powerful marketing tool.

Correspondence typically generated during a job search includes the following:

— Letter that accompanies your résumé, whether in response to an advertisement or a "cold call"

— Letter of request for an informational interview

— "Thank you for the interview" letter

— "Thank you, but no thank you" letter following an interview

— Acceptance or rejection of a job offer

— Letter of request to a reference.

Correspondence samples follow.

REGINALD X. CAPUTO, CPIM, C.P.M.

444 Job Lookers' Drive, Bowling Green, KY 43434

phone: (332) 555-1212   e-mail: RXCap@looking.com

January 29, 1999

Mr. Joseph Black

The Best Company in the World, Inc.

Attn: MATM

1600 Pennsylvania Avenue

Bestown, Ohio 44441

Dear Mr. Black:

I am writing in response to your recent advertisement in the *Bestown Courier* for a Materials Manager. As requested, a copy of my résumé is enclosed for your review.

My background is one of steadily progressive responsibility in plant environments. I possess proven ability, skills, and industry knowledge in materials management, scheduling, purchasing, production, and inventory services, as well as in quality assurance and safety. I have contributed to and led teams whose efforts have resulted in cost containment, impressive cost reductions, and improved operations. I have managed and supervised staff. My adherence to best practices and my personal commitment to professional education have helped to achieve company goals throughout shifts in my employer's management team.

I earned the APICS credential, Certified in Production and Inventory Management (CPIM), in 1994 and will recertify in the coming year. I have completed two of the modules necessary for eventual CIRM certification. I am an APICS-qualified instructor in the body of knowledge of production and inventory management (P&IM), and I have trained groups of up to 40 professionals in P&IM.

Because I want to be associated with an industry leader, I am interested in pursuing this opportunity with you. I can be reached at (332) 555-1212 or via the Internet at rxcap@looking.com.

Sincerely,

Reginald X. Caputo, CPIM, C.P.M.

Enclosure: Résumé

Reginald Caputo, CPIM_____

444 Job Lookers' Drive, Bowling Green, KY 43434

phone: (332) 555-1212   e-mail: RXCap@looking.com

January 29, 1999

Mr. Joseph Black

The Best Company in the World, Inc.

1600 Pennsylvania Avenue

Bestown, Ohio 44441

Dear Mr. Black:

I am an accomplished materials manager who is beginning a job search. A mutual friend of ours, Mike Renfro, suggested I send a copy of my résumé for your review. I would be very appreciative of any insights you could share with me regarding the current job search environment for materials managers.

My assets include proven ability, skills, and industry knowledge in materials management, scheduling, purchasing, production, and inventory services, as well as in quality assurance and safety. I have contributed to and led teams whose efforts have resulted in cost containment, impressive cost reductions, and improved operations. I have managed and supervised staffs ranging in size from 2 to 25. My adherence to best practices and my personal commitment to professional education have helped to achieve company goals throughout well-publicized shifts due to downsizing in my employer's management team.

In addition to earning a Bachelor of Science degree in business administration, I earned the APICS credential, Certified in Production and Inventory Management (CPIM), in 1994 and will recertify in the coming year. I am an APICS-qualified instructor in the body of knowledge of production and inventory management, and I have trained groups of up to 40 professionals in the basics of supply chain management.

Because you work for an industry leader, I am especially interested in any ideas or information you can share. I will call you the week of February 5 to introduce myself and perhaps set a time for meeting with you. Thank you for any assistance you may be able to provide.

Sincerely,

Reginald X. Caputo, CPIM

Enclosure: Résumé

SAMPLE
"THANK YOU
FOR THE
INTERVIEW"
LETTER
(I'M STILL
INTERESTED)

Reginald X. Caputo, Ph.D., CFPIM, CPIM

February 10, 1999

Mr. Joseph Black
The Best Company in the World, Inc.
1600 Pennsylvania Avenue
Bestown, Ohio 44441

Regarding: Materials Manager Position

Dear Joe:

I enjoyed meeting you, having the opportunity to tour the plant, and discussing the Materials Manager position with you yesterday. I found your insight into the challenges and rewards of this opportunity very helpful.

I appreciate your candor regarding the challenges The Best Company is facing in the next two years. I am excited by them! As you know, my experience includes successful ERP implementation, supervision of staff, and facilitation of teams. I believe my successful completion of the course, *Train the Trainer*, and my experience teaching production and inventory management could be assets to The Best Company as it undergoes significant change.

I am very interested in pursuing the Materials Manager position with The Best Company. Should you have any questions, please do not hesitate to call me.

Sincerely,

Reginald X. Caputo, Ph.D., CFPIM, CPIM

444 Job Lookers' Drive, Bowling Green, KY 43434
phone: (332) 555-1212   e-mail: RXCap@looking.com

Reginald X. Caputo, CPA, CPIM

444 Job Lookers' Drive, Bowling Green, KY 43434

phone: (332) 555-1212

e-mail: RXCap@looking.com

February 10, 1999

Mr. Joseph Black
The Best Company in the World, Inc.
1600 Pennsylvania Avenue
Bestown, Ohio 44441

Regarding: Materials Manager Position

Dear Joe:

I enjoyed meeting you yesterday. Having the opportunity to tour the plant and to discuss the Materials Manager position was very beneficial.

I appreciate your candor regarding the challenging opportunities The Best Company is facing. Although I am excited by the corporate opportunities and industry reputation The Best Company offers, I do not believe the Materials Manager position we discussed will make maximum use of my skills and interests. Consequently, I respectfully request that my name be removed from consideration for this position.

Again, I appreciate your time and interest. Should you have any questions, I hope you will not hesitate to call me.

Sincerely,

Reginald X. Caputo, CPA, CPIM

SAMPLE LETTER TO SEND TO A REFERENCE

Reginald X. Caputo, CIRM, CIWA, Jonah

444 Job Lookers' Drive, Bowling Green, KY 43434
phone: (332) 555-1212 e-mail: RXCap@looking.com

January 15, 1999

Lawrence G. Knowledge, Ph.D.
1600 Pennsylvania Avenue
Washington, DC 28370

Dear Larry:

You'll be happy to know that the use of our ERP system has gone as smoothly as the implementation. My experience in planning and executing its implementation remains one of my top three job highlights.

It was a pleasure to discuss my professional goals with you last week. Please know I appreciate the time you spent from a busy day. After careful thought and consideration, I have concluded that one of my goals is to locate new employment that will maximize my experience and interests. I am enclosing a copy of my résumé for your review.

May I use you as a professional reference and refer potential employers to you? I believe you could offer a potential employer valuable insight into my planning and task execution skills, my facilitation and team-building abilities, and my aptitude with new technology.

I, of course, consider this request confidential, just as I would consider your reference confidential. I release you from any liability associated with any reference you give on my behalf.

I will call you later in the week to follow up with this request.

Sincerely,

Reginald X. Caputo, CIRM, CIWA, Jonah
Enclosure: Résumé

6

SECTION 6:
THE INTERVIEW

Section 6:
The Interview

If you've been invited for an interview, Congratulations! Your marketing brochure did its job!

The Phone Call

Consistently use the administrative processes you set in place during your preparatory work. For example, keep a pad and pen by the phone. When the recruiter or other company representative calls to establish a time for an interview, consider the following.

— Have your calendar available so you can readily establish an interview time.

— Ask the caller about the structure of the interview process:

– How much time will be involved?

– Will you be expected to complete skill-based tests?

– Will you be expected to complete personality tests?

– With whom will you be speaking, and what are their positions?

– Will an application be sent out before the interview or will you be completing one when you arrive?

– Is any additional information on the company or job available?

– If considerable travel is involved, will the company be providing either up-front payment or reimbursement of your costs?

– What is the specific title of the position?

– What is the dress policy for the company? If the employer specifies business, business casual, or casual dress, your conformity to the company dress policy could affect your sense of comfort during the interview.

In other words, it's up to you to ensure you are confronted by as few surprises as possible when you arrive at the interview.

PREPARING FOR THE INTERVIEW

Critically review any information sent to you by the employer. What does the employer's information tell you? What does it not tell you?

Use the Internet to scan the company's Web site. Note stock prices, revenue information, new contract information, downsizing announcements, and so forth. Check to see when the site was last updated.

If the employer sends an application, complete it before the interview. Do not write, "see attached résumé," unless the application specifically states that is a permissible action.

Make sure you have correct directions. If possible, make a practice run to the site to ensure you know how much time it will take.

Two days before the interview, call your contact to confirm the time and date of the interview.

Prepare the questions you want to ask of your interviewers.

WHEN YOU ARRIVE AT THE INTERVIEW

The interview should be no different than any other test: preparation is key. Prepare to be under constant scrutiny. Everything you say and do will be reviewed, noticed, and discussed: arrival time, grooming, listening skills, grammatical correctness, application completeness, and testing.

If you are given a name badge, put it on your right shoulder. As you shake hands, you will naturally project your right shoulder toward your interviewer, which will provide an easily accessible visual reminder of your name.

Carry your briefcase in your left hand so that your right hand is free to shake hands.

If you are asked to complete paperwork on site, do so. Do not give the frontline staff or human resources representatives a hard time. They are just doing their jobs. Be aware that it is not uncommon for managers to ask frontline staff how job applicants treated them. Their assessment of your manners, interpersonal skills, and ability to follow directions could affect your evaluation.

A résumé is a marketing document. An application is a legal document. It must be totally accurate. Inaccuracies, omissions, or falsifications may result in your being dismissed from the interview process and, if hired, from employment.

You may be asked to sign a release from an outside firm that is hired to complete background checks. Most common components of that check are verifications of past employment, current employment, educational achievements, credentials earned, salary level, professional certifications, and criminal history. For individuals who have fiscal responsibility, a credit check may also be included. Be 100 percent accurate with all of the information you provide on the application.

INTRODUCTIONS

Stand up. Smile. Speak clearly when introducing yourself.

Make eye contact. Smile. Offer to shake hands.

Offer your business card. Take the business card of everyone you meet so you have correct information available for your post-interview thank-you notes.

DURING THE INTERVIEW

Your goals: (1) to assess if this job fulfills your strategic plan and (2) to assess if this company is one with which you want to associate. Use your prepared questions, and take notes of your interviewer's answers. Look for consistencies and inconsistencies in answers.

The interviewer's goals: (1) to assess whether you are qualified to perform the job successfully and (2) to assess, using his or her knowledge of company culture and known constraints, if you are a good fit for the company.

As the interview progresses, ask questions as they occur to you about the job, work conditions, goals expected, results expected, and so forth.

Keep the interview as conversational as possible.

Again, remember to sit up straight and to breathe! Many applicants report dizziness or slight disorientation during an interview. Oxygen deprivation is at work due to quick, short, shallow breaths. Breathe as normally as possible. Doing so will also help you project an energetic image.

BEHAVIORAL INTERVIEWS AND STRESS INTERVIEWS

Many interviewers use interviewing techniques to look for behavior patterns such as why you take and leave jobs, areas of progressive responsibility, and working relationships. However, you may experience a stress interview at some point, especially if the job duties include working with the public or handling difficult situations. The interviewer is trying to assess how you operate under stress, so relax! Handle a stress interviewer as you would a difficult customer: with poise, tact, strong product knowledge, and active listening skills to ensure you have a complete understanding of the situation.

What distinguishes a stress interview? There will be no easing in to the interview. It will begin in a confrontational manner. Examples of stress interview questions and "appropriate" responses follow.

Question: Mr. Caputo, why do you want this job?

Answer: (Smile) Please call me Reg. At this point in the interview process, I don't have enough information to say whether or not I want this job. I would be very interested in knowing what you see as the pluses and minuses of the job.

Question: I don't read résumés. Tell me what's on yours.

Answer: (Smile) Thanks for the opportunity to talk about myself! I am a manufacturing professional with impressive experience in materials management and purchasing. I have led and contributed to teams that have produced a 300 percent increase in revenue over a three-year period. My analysis realized a $1.2 million cost reduction last year alone. When I took over my current job responsibilities, inventory accuracy was 77.9 percent. Eight months later, I had it to 96 percent, and it has now stabilized at 99.9 percent. I have a college degree in business administration, and I am CPIM certified. I completed training in constraints management last year. I am an active member of APICS, and I train about 100 people a year in supply chain management.

Question: Why should I interview you? I don't think we can afford you.

Answer: That's interesting. The pay scale was advertised in the newspaper, and it was in my range. Has something changed?

or

That's an interesting insight. What do you believe my fair market value is compared with the compensation level set for this job?

QUESTIONS YOU MIGHT BE ASKED

Applicants are generally asked two distinct types of questions: (1) résumé-generated questions that vary from person to person and (2) position-based questions that are asked of every applicant.

Listen to what is asked and respond accurately. If you are asked for three examples, provide your best three examples—not five. If you don't have three examples, acknowledge that, and provide your best one or two examples.

The following questions may be typical from interviewer to interviewer. Some people find it very helpful to practice answering these questions before an interview.

— What aspect of your current (most recent) job has been most challenging? Why?

— Every employee faces challenges every day. Tell me about three challenges you have faced in the past year.

— What is the biggest challenge facing your current employer? How could you be best positioned to positively affect resolution?

— How has your performance contributed to resolving challenges?

— Tell me what you know about this company.

— In your opinion, what are the three most significant challenges facing your profession in the next five years?

— In your opinion, what are the three most significant challenges facing the manufacturing industry in the next five years?

— Give me two examples of how your plant's environment was affected by companywide change.

— Give me two examples of how doing your job was affected by changing work conditions.

— You're involved in a job search, or you wouldn't be here. Describe for me the employment conditions you are looking for in your next work environment.

— What traits do you value in your coworkers?

— What do you look for in your supervisor?

— What is your current employer's strategic mission? How does your job contribute to the company's reaching that mission?

— What strategic planning initiatives have you been involved in?

— Describe your experience in creating/leading/contributing to a cross-functional team.

— Describe the processes you would put in place to ensure that a cross-functional team can work successfully.

— Do you believe accountability and empowerment are connected? Tell me how.

— Drawing from your experience, do you believe it is more important to be fair or to be consistent? Provide examples to support your belief.

— What three words would your peers use to describe your leadership style?

— Describe how supply chain management theory has affected how you do your job.

— Describe how you communicate with your staff/team.

— Describe the best manager you've ever worked for.

— What similarities do your project management skills and your staff management skills share?

— Tell me how you have delegated decision-making authority on a past job.

— Describe three characteristics of a collaborative work style. Follow up: To what degree do you possess those three characteristics?

— Tell me how to establish a timeline for an ERP implementation.

— If your plant manager became ill and you had to step into his or her job for a month, what steps would you take to ensure that business goals continued to be met? Follow up: Whose work would suffer, yours or the manager's?

— Tell me about a time when staff attrition affected your ability to do your job. What did you learn from the experience?

— If you discovered that one of your coworkers had falsified information on the master schedule, what would you do?

— What is the most difficult work situation you've faced? Follow up: With the advantage of 20-20 hindsight, how would you handle the same problem tomorrow?

— If you hear someone say, "A member of my team has an attitude problem," what would the phrase "attitude problem" mean to you?

— How do you educate your staff to your expectations regarding performance and attendance?

— What would you do if you found yourself speaking with a customer who had lost his or her temper? Has this ever happened to you? How did you respond?

— What is your greatest asset among your interpersonal skills?

— Whose people skills do you admire, and why?

— What interpersonal skill needs improvement?

— How are you working toward that improvement?

— Rate yourself as a problem-solver. Give examples that substantiate your rating.

— What's the most unconventional way you've solved a problem?

— What types of problems are you best equipped to solve?

— How do you set your personal performance goals?

— What has been your best educational experience? Why?

— Describe your process for setting performance goals for your staff.

— What do you believe are the three key challenges facing a supervisor, day in and day out?

— What is the Fair Labor Standards Act (FLSA)?
FYI: The FLSA is a federal law that governs overtime compensation; it provides for payment of overtime for every hour worked over 40 hours in a work week at the rate of one and one-half times the regular rate. The FLSA also sets up categories of employees who are conditionally exempt from the overtime regulations: executive, administrative, professional, outside sales, and computer professionals.

— This position will require supervision of exempt and non-exempt staff. Tell me how an employee's eligibility for overtime affects how you supervise.

— Tell me how you would motivate a chronically tardy employee to improve his or her behavior.

— Tell me why managerial consistency across the organization is or is not important.

— Tell me what constitutes sexual harassment.
FYI: There are two types of sexual harassment: (1) quid pro quo, which means a condition of employment is based on providing a sexual favor of some kind, and (2) a hostile work environment.

— What is COBRA?
FYI: COBRA is a federal regulation that provides for the continuation of medical insurance after employment ends, for a specific period of time, at the expense of the former employee.

— What is the Family and Medical Leave Act (FMLA)?

FYI: The FMLA is a federal law that guarantees 12 weeks of job-protected leave to eligible employees to deal with their own serious illness; the serious illness of a child, spouse, or parent; or the birth or adoption of a child.

— How has the FMLA affected your job as a manager?

— What is the Americans with Disabilities Act (ADA)?

FYI: The ADA is a federal law that guarantees equal access to buildings, training, education, and other conditions of employment to individuals with disabilities. The ADA requires employers to make reasonable accommodations to otherwise qualified individuals with disabilities so they can succeed on the job. However, the employer, not the employee, defines what is "reasonable."

— How may the Americans with Disabilities Act (ADA) affect how you manage your staff and your product line?

— Is there any difference between Equal Employment Opportunity (EEO) regulations and Affirmative Action, and, if so, what is it?

FYI: Yes, there is a difference. EEO laws prohibit discrimination against any individual on the basis of a series of protected categories, some of which are age, gender, religion, creed, race, color, national origin, and veteran status. In general, EEO laws were passed in response to cases of overt discrimination against individuals for non-job-related reasons. Affirmative Action, on the other hand, results from an Executive Order that responded to historical and current systemic discrimination against women and minority groups. Certain classes of employers are required to analyze their workforce in terms of actual representation and possible workforce representation of women and members of minority groups.

— Define quality.

FYI: Quality is a measurement of how well you have met requirements. If you have met your requirements, you have produced a quality product or provided a quality service.

— If you could work on any type of product, what would it be and why?

— Are you more interested in product development, product marketing, product sales, or product management?

— I am going to read a list of manufacturing areas. Tell me your two strongest areas and two in which you want more experience. Enterprise Resource Management, Constraints Management, Materials Management, Purchasing, Inventory Management, Pricing, ERP Implementation, MRP, MRP II.

— If you could work for any company, doing any job, what would that be?

— Why should we hire you?

— What questions do you have for me?

QUESTIONS YOU MIGHT ASK

Few things are as disappointing as an applicant who asks no questions of the interviewer. It implies lack of interest in the job and the company. At best, it is rude. At worst, you've lost access to information that could be helpful in making your decision about the job and the company, as well as access to information that could be valuable during the next interview!

The following sample questions might be asked of any interviewer, regardless of his or her role. Always compare the consistency of the answers when you have multiple interviewers.

— For a newly created position: Tell me why this job was created, and what results are expected in the first year.

— For an existing position: Tell me about the two people who had this job most recently. In which areas were they successful? In which areas were they challenged?

— What's the attrition rate for this position? Why is that?

— Why do people leave this position?

— What do you believe is the greatest challenge facing the company in the coming year? The coming three years?

— What is the company's strategic mission? How does this job fit into that mission? How does it help fulfill that mission?

— What positions does this job interact with most? Describe the strength of those relationships. Describe what events may have damaged those relationships in the past three years.

— How often are team meetings held? Are they facilitated? Is an agenda used?

— If you could work for anyone, who would it be and why?

— How do you describe for strangers what this company does?

— Complete this sentence: My job is to…

— How long have you worked here?

— What other positions have you worked in?

— What business areas have been the focus of your career?

— What keeps you here?

— How does the company do its budgeting? Describe the process.

— Describe the company's commitment to lifelong learning.

— What is the training budget for this position?

— When is the fiscal year?

— What are the key components of this position's budget?

— Whom can I count on to help me be successful?

— Is there anyone who has applied for this job internally? How was it left with that person?

— Describe three current staff members you believe are representative of your company's commitment to staff development.

— Describe the character traits most valued by this company.

— How has the company changed since you've been here?

ILLEGAL QUESTIONS

No interviewer may legally ask a question whose answer could be used to make an employment decision on the basis of age, national origin, parental status, marital status, religion, creed, race, ethnic identity, veteran status, or disability status.

Some illegal questions may be asked innocently as ice-breaker questions, such as "Where are you from originally?" However, because the answer to that question could cause you to reveal your national origin, it is an illegal question.

Some illegal questions may be asked specifically to obtain non-job-related information from you. You may always respond, "That's an interesting question. Could you tell me how it is related to employment here?"

Assume that all information you provide during an interview will be used to make a hiring decision. How you respond to any question, even an illegal question, may be a factor in making a hiring decision. It is entirely up to you to decide how to respond to all questions, including illegal questions.

AFTER THE INTERVIEW

Relax. Breathe deeply.

Find a quiet place—your car will do—to write down every question you were asked. If you can, jot down your answers also. Review the list of questions from time to time. Over the course of a few interviews, you may find a pattern emerging in the questions being asked. This pattern should make preparing for each interview easier.

Were any questions difficult to answer? How would you like to handle that question in a future interview?

Decide which issues you want to address in your thank-you notes. Mail these notes within 36 hours of your interview.

Ask yourself: Am I interested in this job? Why?

Ask yourself: Am I interested in this company? Why?

SECTION 7:
MARKETING YOURSELF ON THE INTERNET AND AT CAREER FAIRS

SECTION 7:
MARKETING YOURSELF ON THE INTERNET AND AT CAREER FAIRS

INTERNET-BASED SERVICES

If you decide to use an Internet-based service to apply for a position, follow the formatting guidelines requested by the service. For example, some require a particular type size, font, no use of tabs, no use of boldface, and so forth.

CAREER FAIRS

Before attending a career fair, develop a 10-second introduction of yourself.

If you attend a career fair, bring plenty of résumés. Depending on how many employers are represented and how many levels of interviewers are available on site, you may need 50 or more résumés during one career fair.

Bring your business card, and ask for the business cards of your potential employers' staff. Drop a note of thanks following the fair.

Review published material to know which employers will be present. Rank the employers according to your interest, and visit their sites in the order of your interest.

Review published material regarding the database generated from the event. Employers who attend career fairs usually receive a database that lists every attendee. Sometimes employers who do not attend may purchase this attendee database. If your employer purchases the list, you may want to ensure that your name does not appear on the database. Your decision should be made before the event.

Dress and groom yourself as if you were going to an interview.

Remember: brief case and résumé in your left hand.

Remember: name badge on your right shoulder.

SECTION 8:
THE MARKETING
PROCESS CONTINUES

SECTION 8:
THE MARKETING PROCESS CONTINUES

Enjoy and learn from each aspect of the job-search process. A job search presents a unique opportunity to explore your values, establish a strategic plan for yourself, and control that strategic process.

Always have an up-to-date résumé. Creating a résumé can be very self-affirming, and it's a powerful attachment to an annual "self-appraisal" because it speaks to your values, your professional progress, and your level of employability.

Network at every opportunity. Attend meetings of your professional societies. Remember that there is a difference between secrecy and confidentiality. Your job search cannot remain a secret. However, it can be handled with a degree of confidentiality that encourages appropriate networking.

Be open to constructive criticism. Invite four people to dinner and have them review your latest résumé.

Continue your professional development activities. Read or review a professional journal. Pursue professional certification, and contribute to a study group. Listen to audiotapes. Attend APICS professional development meetings.

Create a presentation on yourself using presentation software. Practice giving it! Again, this is a powerful attachment to your annual performance "appraisal."

Consistently measure your progress, and look for opportunities for continuous improvement.

Build your informational resources. Read the newspaper daily. Scan the Web regularly for information about your profession and industry.

Integrate all that you experience and learn into your job search.